UNITED STATES MODEL INCOME TAX CONVENTION OF SEPTEMBER 20, 1996

```
                    CONVENTION BETWEEN
                THE UNITED STATES OF AMERICA
                       AND -------
         FOR THE AVOIDANCE OF DOUBLE TAXATION AND THE
                PREVENTION OF FISCAL EVASION
                 WITH RESPECT TO TAXES ON INCOME
```

    The United States of America and -----, desiring to conclude
a Convention for the avoidance of double taxation and the
prevention of fiscal evasion with respect to taxes on income,
have agreed as follows:

1996 U.S. Model
Income Tax Convention

Article 1

GENERAL SCOPE

1. This Convention shall apply only to persons who are residents of one or both of the Contracting States, except as otherwise provided in the Convention.

2. The Convention shall not restrict in any manner any benefit now or hereafter accorded:

   a) by the laws of either Contracting State; or

   b) by any other agreement between the Contracting States.

3. Notwithstanding the provisions of subparagraph 2(b):

   (a) the provisions of Article 25(Mutual Agreement Procedure) of this Convention exclusively shall apply to any dispute concerning whether a measure is within the scope of this Convention, and the procedures under this Convention exclusively shall apply to that dispute; and

   (b) unless the competent authorities determine that a taxation measure is not within the scope of this Convention, the nondiscrimination obligations of this Convention exclusively shall apply with respect to that measure, except for such national treatment or most-favored-nation obligations as may apply to trade in goods under the General Agreement on Tariffs and Trade. No national treatment or most-favored-nation obligation under any other agreement shall apply with respect to that measure.

   (c) For the purpose of this paragraph, a "measure" is a law, regulation, rule, procedure, decision, administrative action, or any similar provision or action.

4. Notwithstanding any provision of the Convention except paragraph 5 of this Article, a Contracting State may tax its residents (as determined under Article 4 (Residence)), and by reason of citizenship may tax its citizens, as if the Convention had not come into effect. For this purpose, the term "citizen" shall include a former citizen or long-term resident whose loss of such status had as one of its principal purposes the avoidance

1996 U.S. Model
Income Tax Convention

of tax (as defined under the laws of the Contracting State of which the person was a citizen or long-term resident), but only for a period of 10 years following such loss.

5. The provisions of paragraph 4 shall not affect:

    a) the benefits conferred by a Contracting State under paragraph 2 of Article 9 (Associated Enterprises), paragraphs 2 and 5 of Article 18 (Pensions, Social Security, Annuities, Alimony, and Child Support), and Articles 23 (Relief From Double Taxation), 24 (Non-Discrimination), and 25 (Mutual Agreement Procedure); and

    b) the benefits conferred by a Contracting State under paragraph 6 of Article 18 (Pensions, Social Security, Annuities, Alimony, and Child Support), Articles 19 (Government Service), 20 (Students and Trainees), and 27 (Diplomatic Agents and Consular Officers), upon individuals who are neither citizens of, nor have been admitted for permanent residence in, that State.

1996 U.S. Model
Income Tax Convention

Article 2

TAXES COVERED

1. The existing taxes to which this Convention shall apply are:

    a) in the United States: the Federal income taxes imposed by the Internal Revenue Code (but excluding social security taxes), and the Federal excise taxes imposed with respect to private foundations.

    b) in _____ : _____ .

2. The Convention shall apply also to any identical or substantially similar taxes that are imposed after the date of signature of the Convention in addition to, or in place of, the existing taxes. The competent authorities of the Contracting States shall notify each other of any significant changes that have been made in their respective taxation laws or other laws affecting their obligations under the Convention, and of any official published material concerning the application of the Convention, including explanations, regulations, rulings, or judicial decisions.

1996 U.S. Model
Income Tax Convention

Article 3

GENERAL DEFINITIONS

1. For the purposes of this Convention, unless the context otherwise requires:

a) the term "person" includes an individual, an estate, a trust, a partnership, a company, and any other body of persons;

b) the term "company" means any body corporate or any entity that is treated as a body corporate for tax purposes according to the laws of the state in which it is organized;

c) the terms "enterprise of a Contracting State" and "enterprise of the other Contracting State" mean respectively an enterprise carried on by a resident of a Contracting State, and an enterprise carried on by a resident of the other Contracting State; the terms also include an enterprise carried on by a resident of a Contracting State through an entity that is treated as fiscally transparent in that Contracting State;

d) the term "international traffic" means any transport by a ship or aircraft, except when such transport is solely between places in a Contracting State;

e) the term "competent authority" means:

    (i) in the United States: the Secretary of the Treasury or his delegate; and

    (ii) in _____: _____;

f) the term "United States" means the United States of America, and includes the states thereof and the District of Columbia; such term also includes the territorial sea thereof and the sea bed and subsoil of the submarine areas adjacent to that territorial sea, over which the United States exercises sovereign rights in accordance with international law; the term, however, does not include Puerto Rico, the Virgin Islands, Guam or any other United States possession or territory;

g) the term _____ means _____;

h) the term "national" of a Contracting State, means:

(i) any individual possessing the nationality or citizenship of that State; and

(ii) any legal person, partnership or association deriving its status as such from the laws in force in that State;

i) the term "qualified governmental entity" means:

(i) any person or body of persons that constitutes a governing body of a Contracting State, or of a political subdivision or local authority of a Contracting State;

(ii) a person that is wholly owned, directly or indirectly, by a Contracting State or a political subdivision or local authority of a Contracting State, provided (A) it is organized under the laws of the Contracting State, (B) its earnings are credited to its own account with no portion of its income inuring to the benefit of any private person, and (C) its assets vest in the Contracting State, political subdivision or local authority upon dissolution; and

(iii) a pension trust or fund of a person described in subparagraph (i) or (ii) that is constituted and operated exclusively to administer or provide pension benefits described in Article 19;

provided that an entity described in subparagraph (ii) or (iii) does not carry on commercial activities.

2. As regards the application of the Convention at any time by a Contracting State any term not defined therein shall, unless the context otherwise requires, or the competent authorities agree to a common meaning pursuant to the provisions of Article 25 (Mutual Agreement Procedure), have the meaning which it has at that time under the law of that State for the purposes of the taxes to which the Convention applies, any meaning under the applicable tax laws of that State prevailing over a meaning given to the term under other laws of that State.

1996 U.S. Model
Income Tax Convention

Article 4

RESIDENCE

1. Except as provided in this paragraph, for the purposes of this Convention, the term "resident of a Contracting State" means any person who, under the laws of that State, is liable to tax therein by reason of his domicile, residence, citizenship, place of management, place of incorporation, or any other criterion of a similar nature.

    a) The term "resident of a Contracting State" does not include any person who is liable to tax in that State in respect only of income from sources in that State or of profits attributable to a permanent establishment in that State.

    b) A legal person organized under the laws of a Contracting State and that is generally exempt from tax in that State and is established and maintained in that State either:

        i) exclusively for a religious, charitable, educational, scientific, or other similar purpose; or

        ii) to provide pensions or other similar benefits to employees pursuant to a plan

is to be treated for purposes of this paragraph as a resident of that Contracting State.

    c) A qualified governmental entity is to be treated as a resident of the Contracting State where it is established.

    d) An item of income, profit or gain derived through an entity that is fiscally transparent under the laws of either Contracting State shall be considered to be derived by a resident of a State to the extent that the item is treated for purposes of the taxation law of such Contracting State as the income, profit or gain of a resident.

2. Where by reason of the provisions of paragraph 1, an individual is a resident of both Contracting States, then his status shall be determined as follows:

a) he shall be deemed to be a resident of the State in which he has a permanent home available to him; if he has a permanent home available to him in both States, he shall be deemed to be a resident of the State with which his personal and economic relations are closer (center of vital interests);

b) if the State in which he has his center of vital interests cannot be determined, or if he does not have a permanent home available to him in either State, he shall be deemed to be a resident of the State in which he has an habitual abode;

c) if he has an habitual abode in both States or in neither of them, he shall be deemed to be a resident of the State of which he is a national;

d) if he is a national of both States or of neither of them, the competent authorities of the Contracting States shall endeavor to settle the question by mutual agreement.

3. Where by reason of the provisions of paragraph 1 a company is a resident of both Contracting States, then if it is created under the laws of one of the Contracting States or a political subdivision thereof, it shall be deemed to be a resident of that State.

4. Where by reason of the provisions of paragraph 1 a person other than an individual or a company is a resident of both Contracting States, the competent authorities of the Contracting States shall endeavor to settle the question by mutual agreement and determine the mode of application of the Convention to such person.

1996 U.S. Model
Income Tax Convention

Article 5

PERMANENT ESTABLISHMENT

1. For the purposes of this Convention, the term "permanent establishment" means a fixed place of business through which the business of an enterprise is wholly or partly carried on.

2. The term "permanent establishment" includes especially:

   a) a place of management;

   b) a branch;

   c) an office;

   d) a factory;

   e) a workshop; and

   f) a mine, an oil or gas well, a quarry, or any other place of extraction of natural resources.

3. A building site or construction or installation project, or an installation or drilling rig or ship used for the exploration of natural resources, constitutes a permanent establishment only if it lasts or the activity continues for more than twelve months.

4. Notwithstanding the preceding provisions of this Article, the term "permanent establishment" shall be deemed not to include:

   a) the use of facilities solely for the purpose of storage, display or delivery of goods or merchandise belonging to the enterprise;

   b) the maintenance of a stock of goods or merchandise belonging to the enterprise solely for the purpose of storage, display or delivery;

   c) the maintenance of a stock of goods or merchandise belonging to the enterprise solely for the purpose of processing by another enterprise;

d) the maintenance of a fixed place of business solely for the purpose of purchasing goods or merchandise, or of collecting information, for the enterprise;

e) the maintenance of a fixed place of business solely for the purpose of carrying on, for the enterprise, any other activity of a preparatory or auxiliary character;

f) the maintenance of a fixed place of business solely for any combination of the activities mentioned in subparagraphs a) through e).

5. Notwithstanding the provisions of paragraphs 1 and 2, where a person -- other than an agent of an independent status to whom paragraph 6 applies -- is acting on behalf of an enterprise and has and habitually exercises in a Contracting State an authority to conclude contracts that are binding on the enterprise, that enterprise shall be deemed to have a permanent establishment in that State in respect of any activities that the person undertakes for the enterprise, unless the activities of such person are limited to those mentioned in paragraph 4 that, if exercised through a fixed place of business, would not make this fixed place of business a permanent establishment under the provisions of that paragraph.

6. An enterprise shall not be deemed to have a permanent establishment in a Contracting State merely because it carries on business in that State through a broker, general commission agent, or any other agent of an independent status, provided that such persons are acting in the ordinary course of their business as independent agents.

7. The fact that a company that is a resident of a Contracting State controls or is controlled by a company that is a resident of the other Contracting State, or that carries on business in that other State (whether through a permanent establishment or otherwise), shall not constitute either company a permanent establishment of the other.

1996 U.S. Model
Income Tax Convention

Article 6

INCOME FROM REAL PROPERTY (IMMOVABLE PROPERTY)

1. Income derived by a resident of a Contracting State from real property (immovable property), including income from agriculture or forestry, situated in the other Contracting State may be taxed in that other State.

2. The term "real property (immovable property)" shall have the meaning which it has under the law of the Contracting State in which the property in question is situated.

3. The provisions of paragraph 1 shall apply to income derived from the direct use, letting, or use in any other form of real property.

4. The provisions of paragraphs 1 and 3 shall also apply to the income from real property of an enterprise and to income from real property used for the performance of independent personal services.

5. A resident of a Contracting State who is liable to tax in the other Contracting State on income from real property situated in the other Contracting State may elect for any taxable year to compute the tax on such income on a net basis as if such income were business profits attributable to a permanent establishment in such other State. Any such election shall be binding for the taxable year of the election and all subsequent taxable years unless the competent authority of the Contracting State in which the property is situated agrees to terminate the election.

1996 U.S. Model
Income Tax Convention

Article 7

BUSINESS PROFITS

1. The business profits of an enterprise of a Contracting State shall be taxable only in that State unless the enterprise carries on business in the other Contracting State through a permanent establishment situated therein. If the enterprise carries on business as aforesaid, the business profits of the enterprise may be taxed in the other State but only so much of them as are attributable to that permanent establishment.

2. Subject to the provisions of paragraph 3, where an enterprise of a Contracting State carries on business in the other Contracting State through a permanent establishment situated therein, there shall in each Contracting State be attributed to that permanent establishment the business profits that it might be expected to make if it were a distinct and independent enterprise engaged in the same or similar activities under the same or similar conditions. For this purpose, the business profits to be attributed to the permanent establishment shall include only the profits derived from the assets or activities of the permanent establishment.

3. In determining the business profits of a permanent establishment, there shall be allowed as deductions expenses that are incurred for the purposes of the permanent establishment, including a reasonable allocation of executive and general administrative expenses, research and development expenses, interest, and other expenses incurred for the purposes of the enterprise as a whole (or the part thereof which includes the permanent establishment), whether incurred in the State in which the permanent establishment is situated or elsewhere.

4. No business profits shall be attributed to a permanent establishment by reason of the mere purchase by that permanent establishment of goods or merchandise for the enterprise.

5. For the purposes of the preceding paragraphs, the profits to be attributed to the permanent establishment shall be determined by the same method of accounting year by year unless there is good and sufficient reason to the contrary.

6. Where business profits include items of income that are dealt with separately in other Articles of the Convention, then

the provisions of those Articles shall not be affected by the provisions of this Article.

7. For the purposes of the Convention, the term "business profits" means income from any trade or business, including income derived by an enterprise from the performance of personal services, and from the rental of tangible personal property.

8. In applying paragraphs 1 and 2 of Article 7 (Business Profits), paragraph 6 of Article 10 (Dividends), paragraph 3 of Article 11 (Interest), paragraph 3 of Article 12 (Royalties), paragraph 3 of Article 13 (Gains), Article 14 (Independent Personal Services) and paragraph 2 of Article 21 (Other Income), any income or gain attributable to a permanent establishment or fixed base during its existence is taxable in the Contracting State where such permanent establishment or fixed base is situated even if the payments are deferred until such permanent establishment or fixed base has ceased to exist.

1996 U.S. Model
Income Tax Convention

Article 8

SHIPPING AND AIR TRANSPORT

1. Profits of an enterprise of a Contracting State from the operation of ships or aircraft in international traffic shall be taxable only in that State.

2. For the purposes of this Article, profits from the operation of ships or aircraft include profits derived from the rental of ships or aircraft on a full (time or voyage) basis. They also include profits from the rental of ships or aircraft on a bareboat basis if such ships or aircraft are operated in international traffic by the lessee, or if the rental income is incidental to profits from the operation of ships or aircraft in international traffic. Profits derived by an enterprise from the inland transport of property or passengers within either Contracting State, shall be treated as profits from the operation of ships or aircraft in international traffic if such transport is undertaken as part of international traffic.

3. Profits of an enterprise of a Contracting State from the use, maintenance, or rental of containers (including trailers, barges, and related equipment for the transport of containers) used in international traffic shall be taxable only in that State.

4. The provisions of paragraphs 1 and 3 shall also apply to profits from participation in a pool, a joint business, or an international operating agency.

1996 U.S. Model
Income Tax Convention

Article 9

ASSOCIATED ENTERPRISES

1. Where:

    a) an enterprise of a Contracting State participates directly or indirectly in the management, control or capital of an enterprise of the other Contracting State; or

    b) the same persons participate directly or indirectly in the management, control, or capital of an enterprise of a Contracting State and an enterprise of the other Contracting State,

and in either case conditions are made or imposed between the two enterprises in their commercial or financial relations that differ from those that would be made between independent enterprises, then, any profits that, but for those conditions, would have accrued to one of the enterprises, but by reason of those conditions have not so accrued, may be included in the profits of that enterprise and taxed accordingly.

2. Where a Contracting State includes in the profits of an enterprise of that State, and taxes accordingly, profits on which an enterprise of the other Contracting State has been charged to tax in that other State, and the other Contracting State agrees that the profits so included are profits that would have accrued to the enterprise of the first-mentioned State if the conditions made between the two enterprises had been those that would have been made between independent enterprises, then that other State shall make an appropriate adjustment to the amount of the tax charged therein on those profits. In determining such adjustment, due regard shall be paid to the other provisions of this Convention and the competent authorities of the Contracting States shall if necessary consult each other.

Article 10

DIVIDENDS

1. Dividends paid by a resident of a Contracting State to a resident of the other Contracting State may be taxed in that other State.

2. However, such dividends may also be taxed in the Contracting State of which the payor is a resident and according to the laws of that State, but if the dividends are beneficially owned by a resident of the other Contracting State, except as otherwise provided, the tax so charged shall not exceed:

   a) 5 percent of the gross amount of the dividends if the beneficial owner is a company that owns directly at least 10 percent of the voting stock of the company paying the dividends;

   b) 15 percent of the gross amount of the dividends in all other cases.

This paragraph shall not affect the taxation of the company in respect of the profits out of which the dividends are paid.

3. Subparagraph a) of paragraph 2 shall not apply in the case of dividends paid by a United States person that is a Regulated Investment Company or a Real Estate Investment Trust (REIT). In the case of a United States person that is a REIT, subparagraph b) of paragraph 2 also shall not apply, unless the dividend is beneficially owned by an individual holding a less than 10-percent interest in the REIT.

4. Notwithstanding paragraph 2, dividends may not be taxed in the Contracting State of which the payor is a resident if the beneficial owner of the dividends is a resident of the other Contracting State that is a qualified governmental entity that does not control the payor of the dividend.

5. For purposes of the Convention, the term "dividends" means income from shares or other rights, not being debt-claims, participating in profits, as well as income that is subjected to the same taxation treatment as income from shares under the laws of the State of which the payor is a resident.

1996 U.S. Model
Income Tax Convention

6. The provisions of paragraphs 1 and 2 shall not apply if the beneficial owner of the dividends, being a resident of a Contracting State, carries on business in the other Contracting State, of which the payor is a resident, through a permanent establishment situated therein, or performs in that other State independent personal services from a fixed base situated therein, and the dividends are attributable to such permanent establishment or fixed base. In such case the provisions of Article 7 (Business Profits) or Article 14 (Independent Personal Services), as the case may be, shall apply.

7. A Contracting State may not impose any tax on dividends paid by a resident of the other State, except insofar as the dividends are paid to a resident of the first-mentioned State or the dividends are attributable to a permanent establishment or a fixed base situated in that State, nor may it impose tax on a corporation's undistributed profits, except as provided in paragraph 8, even if the dividends paid or the undistributed profits consist wholly or partly of profits or income arising in that State.

8. A corporation that is a resident of one of the States and that has a permanent establishment in the other State or that is subject to tax in the other State on a net basis on its income that may be taxed in the other State under Article 6 (Income from Real Property (Immoveable Property)) or under paragraph 1 of Article 13 (Gains) may be subject in that other State to a tax in addition to the tax allowable under the other provisions of this Convention. Such tax, however, may be imposed on only the portion of the business profits of the corporation attributable to the permanent establishment and the portion of the income referred to in the preceding sentence that is subject to tax under Article 6 (Income from Real Property (Immoveable Property)) or under paragraph 1 of Article 13 (Gains) that, in the case of the United States, represents the dividend equivalent amount of such profits or income and, in the case of _____, is an amount that is analogous to the dividend equivalent amount.

9. The tax referred to in paragraph 8 may not be imposed at a rate in excess of the rate specified in paragraph 2 a).

1996 U.S. Model
Income Tax Convention

Article 11

INTEREST

1. Interest arising in a Contracting State and beneficially owned by a resident of the other Contracting State may be taxed only in that other State.

2. The term "interest" as used in this Convention means income from debt-claims of every kind, whether or not secured by mortgage, and whether or not carrying a right to participate in the debtor's profits, and in particular, income from government securities and income from bonds or debentures, including premiums or prizes attaching to such securities, bonds or debentures, and all other income that is subjected to the same taxation treatment as income from money lent by the taxation law of the Contracting State in which the income arises. Income dealt with in Article 10 (Dividends) and penalty charges for late payment shall not be regarded as interest for the purposes of this Convention.

3. The provisions of paragraph 1 shall not apply if the beneficial owner of the interest, being a resident of a Contracting State, carries on business in the other Contracting State, in which the interest arises, through a permanent establishment situated therein, or performs in that other State independent personal services from a fixed base situated therein, and the interest is attributable to such permanent establishment or fixed base. In such case the provisions of Article 7 (Business Profits) or Article 14 (Independent Personal Services), as the case may be, shall apply.

4. Where, by reason of a special relationship between the payer and the beneficial owner or between both of them and some other person, the amount of the interest, having regard to the debt-claim for which it is paid, exceeds the amount which would have been agreed upon by the payer and the beneficial owner in the absence of such relationship, the provisions of this Article shall apply only to the last-mentioned amount. In such case the excess part of the payments shall remain taxable according to the laws of each State, due regard being had to the other provisions of this Convention.

5. Notwithstanding the provisions of paragraph 1:

a) interest paid by a resident of a Contracting State and that is determined with reference to receipts, sales, income, profits or other cash flow of the debtor or a related person, to any change in the value of any property of the debtor or a related person or to any dividend, partnership distribution or similar payment made by the debtor to a related person, and paid to a resident of the other State also may be taxed in the Contracting State in which it arises, and according to the laws of that State, but if the beneficial owner is a resident of the other Contracting State, the gross amount of the interest may be taxed at a rate not exceeding the rate prescribed in subparagraph b) of paragraph 2 of Article 10 (Dividends); and

b) Interest that is an excess inclusion with respect to a residual interest in a real estate mortgage investment conduit may be taxed by each State in accordance with its domestic law.

1996 U.S. Model
Income Tax Convention

Article 12

ROYALTIES

1. Royalties arising in a Contracting State and beneficially owned by a resident of the other Contracting State may be taxed only in that other State.

2. The term "royalties" as used in this Convention means:

    (a) any consideration for the use of, or the right to use, any copyright of literary, artistic, scientific or other work (including computer software, cinematographic films, audio or video tapes or disks, and other means of image or sound reproduction), any patent, trademark, design or model, plan, secret formula or process, or other like right or property, or for information concerning industrial, commercial, or scientific experience; and

    (b) gain derived from the alienation of any property described in subparagraph (a), provided that such gain is contingent on the productivity, use, or disposition of the property.

3. The provisions of paragraph 1 shall not apply if the beneficial owner of the royalties, being a resident of a Contracting State, carries on business in the other Contracting State through a permanent establishment situated therein, or performs in that other State independent personal services from a fixed base situated therein, and the royalties are attributable to such permanent establishment or fixed base. In such case the provisions of Article 7 (Business Profits) or Article 14 (Independent Personal Services), as the case may be, shall apply.

4. Where, by reason of a special relationship between the payer and the beneficial owner or between both of them and some other person, the amount of the royalties, having regard to the use, right, or information for which they are paid, exceeds the amount which would have been agreed upon by the payer and the beneficial owner in the absence of such relationship, the provisions of this Article shall apply only to the last-mentioned amount. In such case the excess part of the payments shall remain taxable according to the laws of each Contracting State, due regard being had to the other provisions of the Convention.

1996 U.S. Model
Income Tax Convention

Article 13

GAINS

1. Gains derived by a resident of a Contracting State that are attributable to the alienation of real property situated in the other Contracting State may be taxed in that other State.

2. For the purposes of this Convention the term "real property situated in the other Contracting State" shall include:

   a) real property referred to in Article 6 (Income from Real Property (Immovable Property));

   b) a United States real property interest; and

   c) an equivalent interest in real property situated in _____.

3. Gains from the alienation of personal property that are attributable to a permanent establishment that an enterprise of a Contracting State has in the other Contracting State, or that are attributable to a fixed base that is available to a resident of a Contracting State in the other Contracting State for the purpose of performing independent personal services, and gains from the alienation of such a permanent establishment (alone or with the whole enterprise) or of such a fixed base, may be taxed in that other State.

4. Gains derived by an enterprise of a Contracting State from the alienation of ships, aircraft, or containers operated or used in international traffic or personal property pertaining to the operation or use of such ships, aircraft, or containers shall be taxable only in that State.

5. Gains from the alienation of any property other than property referred to in paragraphs 1 through 4 shall be taxable only in the Contracting State of which the alienator is a resident.

Article 14

INDEPENDENT PERSONAL SERVICES

1. Income derived by an individual who is a resident of a Contracting State in respect of the performance of personal services of an independent character shall be taxable only in that State, unless the individual has a fixed base regularly available to him in the other Contracting State for the purpose of performing his activities. If he has such a fixed base, the income attributable to the fixed base that is derived in respect of services performed in that other State also may be taxed by that other State.

2. For purposes of paragraph 1, the income that is taxable in the other Contracting State shall be determined under the principles of paragraph 3 of Article 7.

1996 U.S. Model
Income Tax Convention

Article 15

DEPENDENT PERSONAL SERVICES

1. Subject to the provisions of Articles 16 (Directors' Fees), 18 (Pensions, Social Security, Annuities, Alimony, and Child Support) and 19 (Government Service), salaries, wages, and other remuneration derived by a resident of a Contracting State in respect of an employment shall be taxable only in that State unless the employment is exercised in the other Contracting State. If the employment is so exercised, such remuneration as is derived therefrom may be taxed in that other State.

2. Notwithstanding the provisions of paragraph 1, remuneration derived by a resident of a Contracting State in respect of an employment exercised in the other Contracting State shall be taxable only in the first-mentioned State if:

    a) the recipient is present in the other State for a period or periods not exceeding in the aggregate 183 days in any twelve month period commencing or ending in the taxable year concerned;

    b) the remuneration is paid by, or on behalf of, an employer who is not a resident of the other State; and

    c) the remuneration is not borne by a permanent establishment or a fixed base which the employer has in the other State.

3. Notwithstanding the preceding provisions of this Article, remuneration described in paragraph 1 that is derived by a resident of a Contracting State in respect of an employment as a member of the regular complement of a ship or aircraft operated in international traffic shall be taxable only in that State.

Article 16

DIRECTORS' FEES

Directors' fees and other compensation derived by a resident of a Contracting State for services rendered in the other Contracting State in his capacity as a member of the board of directors of a company that is a resident of the other Contracting State may be taxed in that other Contracting State.

1996 U.S. Model
Income Tax Convention

Article 17

ARTISTES AND SPORTSMEN

1. Income derived by a resident of a Contracting State as an entertainer, such as a theater, motion picture, radio, or television artiste, or a musician, or as a sportsman, from his personal activities as such exercised in the other Contracting State, which income would be exempt from tax in that other Contracting State under the provisions of Articles 14 (Independent Personal Services) and 15 (Dependent Personal Services) may be taxed in that other State, except where the amount of the gross receipts derived by such entertainer or sportsman, including expenses reimbursed to him or borne on his behalf, from such activities does not exceed twenty thousand United States dollars ($20,000) or its equivalent in _____ for the taxable year concerned.

2. Where income in respect of activities exercised by an entertainer or a sportsman in his capacity as such accrues not to the entertainer or sportsman himself but to another person, that income, notwithstanding the provisions of Articles 7 (Business Profits) and 14 (Independent Personal Services), may be taxed in the Contracting State in which the activities of the entertainer or sportsman are exercised, unless it is established that neither the entertainer or sportsman nor persons related thereto participate directly or indirectly in the profits of that other person in any manner, including the receipt of deferred remuneration, bonuses, fees, dividends, partnership distributions, or other distributions.

Article 18

PENSIONS, SOCIAL SECURITY, ANNUITIES, ALIMONY, AND CHILD SUPPORT

1. Subject to the provisions of Article 19 (Government Service), pension distributions and other similar remuneration beneficially owned by a resident of a Contracting State, whether paid periodically or as a single sum, shall be taxable only in that State, but only to the extent not included in taxable income in the other Contracting State prior to the distribution.

2. Notwithstanding the provisions of paragraph 1, payments made by a Contracting State under provisions of the social security or similar legislation of that State to a resident of the other Contracting State or to a citizen of the United States shall be taxable only in the first-mentioned State.

3. Annuities derived and beneficially owned by an individual resident of a Contracting State shall be taxable only in that State. The term "annuities" as used in this paragraph means a stated sum paid periodically at stated times during a specified number of years, under an obligation to make the payments in return for adequate and full consideration (other than services rendered).

4. Alimony paid by a resident of a Contracting State, and deductible therein, to a resident of the other Contracting State shall be taxable only in that other State. The term "alimony" as used in this paragraph means periodic payments made pursuant to a written separation agreement or a decree of divorce, separate maintenance, or compulsory support, which payments are taxable to the recipient under the laws of the State of which he is a resident.

5. Periodic payments, not dealt with in paragraph 4, for the support of a child made pursuant to a written separation agreement or a decree of divorce, separate maintenance, or compulsory support, paid by a resident of a Contracting State to a resident of the other Contracting State, shall be exempt from tax in both Contracting States.

6. For purposes of this Convention, where an individual who is a participant in a pension plan that is established and

recognized under the legislation of one of the Contracting States performs personal services in the other Contracting State:

    a) Contributions paid by or on behalf of the individual to the plan during the period that he performs such services in the other State shall be deductible (or excludible) in computing his taxable income in that State. Any benefits accrued under the plan or payments made to the plan by or on behalf of his employer during that period shall not be treated as part of the employee's taxable income and shall be allowed as a deduction in computing the profits of his employer in that other State.

    b) Income earned but not distributed by the plan shall not be taxable in the other State until such time and to the extent that a distribution is made from the plan.

    c) Distributions from the plan to the individual shall not be subject to taxation in the other Contracting State if the individual contributes such amounts to a similar plan established in the other State within a time period and in accordance with any other requirements imposed under the laws of the other State.

    d) The provisions of this paragraph shall not apply unless:

        (i) contributions by or on behalf of the individual to the plan (or to another similar plan for which this plan was substituted) were made before he arrived in the other State; and

        (ii) the competent authority of the other State has agreed that the pension plan generally corresponds to a pension plan recognized for tax purposes by that State.

The benefits granted under this paragraph shall not exceed the benefits that would be allowed by the other State to its residents for contributions to, or benefits otherwise accrued under a pension plan recognized for tax purposes by that State.

Article 19

GOVERNMENT SERVICE

1. Notwithstanding the provisions of Articles 14 (Independent Personal Services), 15 (Dependent Personal Services), 16 (Director's Fees) and 17 (Artistes and Sportsmen):

    a) Salaries, wages and other remuneration, other than a pension, paid from the public funds of a Contracting State or a political subdivision or a local authority thereof to an individual in respect of services rendered to that State or subdivision or authority in the discharge of functions of a governmental nature shall, subject to the provisions of subparagraph (b), be taxable only in that State;

    b) such remuneration, however, shall be taxable only in the other Contracting State if the services are rendered in that State and the individual is a resident of that State who:

        i) is a national of that State; or

        ii) did not become a resident of that State solely for the purpose of rendering the services.

2. Notwithstanding the provisions of paragraph 1 of Article 18 (Pensions, Social Security, Annuities, Alimony, and Child Support):

    a) any pension paid from the public funds of a Contracting State or a political subdivision or a local authority thereof to an individual in respect of services rendered to that State or subdivision or authority in the discharge of functions of a governmental nature shall, subject to the provisions of subparagraph (b), be taxable only in that State;

    b) such pension, however, shall be taxable only in the other Contracting State if the individual is a resident of, and a national of, that State.

1996 U.S. Model
Income Tax Convention

Article 20

STUDENTS AND TRAINEES

Payments received by a student, apprentice, or business trainee who is, or was immediately before visiting a Contracting State, a resident of the other Contracting State, and who is present in the first-mentioned State for the purpose of his full-time education at an accredited educational institution, or for his full-time training, shall not be taxed in that State, provided that such payments arise outside that State, and are for the purpose of his maintenance, education or training. The exemption from tax provided by this Article shall apply to an apprentice or business trainee only for a period of time not exceeding one year from the date he first arrives in the first-mentioned Contracting State for the purpose of his training.

1996 U.S. Model
Income Tax Convention

Article 21

OTHER INCOME

1. Items of income beneficially owned by a resident of a Contracting State, wherever arising, not dealt with in the foregoing Articles of this Convention shall be taxable only in that State.

2. The provisions of paragraph 1 shall not apply to income, other than income from real property as defined in paragraph 2 of Article 6 (Income from Real Property (Immovable Property)), if the beneficial owner of the income, being a resident of a Contracting State, carries on business in the other Contracting State through a permanent establishment situated therein, or performs in that other State independent personal services from a fixed base situated therein, and the income is attributable to such permanent establishment or fixed base. In such case the provisions of Article 7 (Business Profits) or Article 14 (Independent Personal Services), as the case may be, shall apply.

1996 U.S. Model
Income Tax Convention

Article 22

LIMITATION ON BENEFITS

1. A resident of a Contracting State shall be entitled to benefits otherwise accorded to residents of a Contracting State by this Convention only to the extent provided in this Article.

2. A resident of a Contracting State shall be entitled to all the benefits of this Convention if the resident is:

   a) an individual;

   b) a qualified governmental entity;

   c) a company, if

   i) all the shares in the class or classes of shares representing more than 50 percent of the voting power and value of the company are regularly traded on a recognized stock exchange, or

   ii) at least 50 percent of each class of shares in the company is owned directly or indirectly by companies entitled to benefits under clause i), provided that in the case of indirect ownership, each intermediate owner is a person entitled to benefits of the Convention under this paragraph;

   d) described in subparagraph 1(b)(i) of Article 4 (Residence);

   e) described in subparagraph 1(b)(ii) of Article 4 (Residence), provided that more than 50 percent of the person's beneficiaries, members or participants are individuals resident in either Contracting State; or

   f) a person other than an individual, if:

   i) On at least half the days of the taxable year persons described in subparagraphs a), b), c), d) or e) own, directly or indirectly (through a chain of ownership in which each person is entitled to benefits of the Convention under this paragraph), at least 50 percent of each class of shares or other beneficial interests in the person, and

ii) less than 50 percent of the person's gross income for the taxable year is paid or accrued, directly or indirectly, to persons who are not residents of either Contracting State (unless the payment is attributable to a permanent establishment situated in either State), in the form of payments that are deductible for income tax purposes in the person's State of residence.

3. a) A resident of a Contracting State not otherwise entitled to benefits shall be entitled to the benefits of this Convention with respect to an item of income derived from the other State, if:

i) the resident is engaged in the active conduct of a trade or business in the first-mentioned State,

ii) the income is connected with or incidental to the trade or business, and

iii) the trade or business is substantial in relation to the activity in the other State generating the income.

b) For purposes of this paragraph, the business of making or managing investments will not be considered an active trade or business unless the activity is banking, insurance or securities activity conducted by a bank, insurance company or registered securities dealer.

c) Whether a trade or business is substantial for purposes of this paragraph will be determined based on all the facts and circumstances. In any case, however, a trade or business will be deemed substantial if, for the preceding taxable year, or for the average of the three preceding taxable years, the asset value, the gross income, and the payroll expense that are related to the trade or business in the first-mentioned State equal at least 7.5 percent of the resident's (and any related parties') proportionate share of the asset value, gross income and payroll expense, respectively, that are related to the activity that generated the income in the other State, and the average of the three ratios exceeds 10 percent.

d) Income is derived in connection with a trade or business if the activity in the other State generating the

1996 U.S. Model
Income Tax Convention

income is a line of business that forms a part of or is complementary to the trade or business. Income is incidental to a trade or business if it facilitates the conduct of the trade or business in the other State.

4. A resident of a Contracting State not otherwise entitled to benefits may be granted benefits of the Convention if the competent authority of the State from which benefits are claimed so determines.

5. For purposes of this Article the term "recognized stock exchange" means:

a) the NASDAQ System owned by the National Association of Securities Dealers, Inc. and any stock exchange registered with the U.S. Securities and Exchange Commission as a national securities exchange under the U.S. Securities Exchange Act of 1934; and

b) [stock exchanges of the other Contracting State].

1996 U.S. Model
Income Tax Convention

Article 23

RELIEF FROM DOUBLE TAXATION

1. In accordance with the provisions and subject to the limitations of the law of the United States (as it may be amended from time to time without changing the general principle hereof), the United States shall allow to a resident or citizen of the United States as a credit against the United States tax on income

    a) the income tax paid or accrued to _____ by or on behalf of such citizen or resident; and

    b) in the case of a United States company owning at least 10 percent of the voting stock of a company that is a resident of _____ and from which the United States company receives dividends, the income tax paid or accrued to _____ by or on behalf of the payor with respect to the profits out of which the dividends are paid.

For the purposes of this paragraph, the taxes referred to in paragraphs 1(b) and 2 of Article 2 (Taxes Covered) shall be considered income taxes.

2. In accordance with the provisions and subject to the limitations of the law of _____ (as it may be amended from time to time without changing the general principle hereof), _____ shall allow to a resident or citizen of _____ as a credit against the _____ tax on income

    a) the income tax paid or accrued to the United States by or on behalf of such resident of citizen; and

    b) in the case of a _____ company owning at least 10 percent of the voting stock of a company that is a resident of the United States and from which the _____ company receives dividends, the income tax paid or accrued to the United States by or on behalf of the payor with respect to the profits out of which the dividends are paid.

For the purposes of this paragraph, the taxes referred to in paragraphs 1(a) and 2 of Article 2 (Taxes Covered) shall be considered income taxes.

3. Where a United States citizen is a resident of _____:

1996 U.S. Model
Income Tax Convention

a) with respect to items of income that under the provisions of this Convention are exempt from United States tax or that are subject to a reduced rate of United States tax when derived by a resident of _____ who is not a United States citizen, _____ shall allow as a credit against _____ tax, only the tax paid, if any, that the United States may impose under the provisions of this Convention, other than taxes that may be imposed solely by reason of citizenship under the saving clause of paragraph 4 of Article 1 (General Scope);

b) for purposes of computing United States tax on those items of income referred to in subparagraph (a), the United States shall allow as a credit against United States tax the income tax paid to _____ after the credit referred to in subparagraph (a); the credit so allowed shall not reduce the portion of the United States tax that is creditable against the _____ tax in accordance with subparagraph (a); and

c) for the exclusive purpose of relieving double taxation in the United States under subparagraph (b), items of income referred to in subparagraph (a) shall be deemed to arise in _____ to the extent necessary to avoid double taxation of such income under subparagraph (b).

1996 U.S. Model
Income Tax Convention

Article 24

NON-DISCRIMINATION

1. Nationals of a Contracting State shall not be subjected in the other Contracting State to any taxation or any requirement connected therewith that is more burdensome than the taxation and connected requirements to which nationals of that other State in the same circumstances, particularly with respect to taxation on worldwide income, are or may be subjected. This provision shall also apply to persons who are not residents of one or both of the Contracting States.

2. The taxation on a permanent establishment or fixed base that a resident or enterprise of a Contracting State has in the other Contracting State shall not be less favorably levied in that other State than the taxation levied on enterprises or residents of that other State carrying on the same activities. The provisions of this paragraph shall not be construed as obliging a Contracting State to grant to residents of the other Contracting State any personal allowances, reliefs, and reductions for taxation purposes on account of civil status or family responsibilities that it grants to its own residents.

3. Except where the provisions of paragraph 1 of Article 9 (Associated Enterprises), paragraph 4 of Article 11 (Interest), or paragraph 4 of Article 12 (Royalties) apply, interest, royalties, and other disbursements paid by a resident of a Contracting State to a resident of the other Contracting State shall, for the purpose of determining the taxable profits of the first-mentioned resident, be deductible under the same conditions as if they had been paid to a resident of the first-mentioned State. Similarly, any debts of a resident of a Contracting State to a resident of the other Contracting State shall, for the purpose of determining the taxable capital of the first-mentioned resident, be deductible under the same conditions as if they had been contracted to a resident of the first-mentioned State.

4. Enterprises of a Contracting State, the capital of which is wholly or partly owned or controlled, directly or indirectly, by one or more residents of the other Contracting State, shall not be subjected in the first-mentioned State to any taxation or any requirement connected therewith that is more burdensome than the taxation and connected requirements to which other similar enterprises of the first-mentioned State are or may be subjected.

1996 U.S. Model
Income Tax Convention

5. Nothing in this Article shall be construed as preventing either Contracting State from imposing a tax as described in paragraph 8 of Article 10 (Dividends).

6. The provisions of this Article shall, notwithstanding the provisions of Article 2 (Taxes Covered), apply to taxes of every kind and description imposed by a Contracting State or a political subdivision or local authority thereof.

1996 U.S. Model
Income Tax Convention

Article 25

MUTUAL AGREEMENT PROCEDURE

1. Where a person considers that the actions of one or both of the Contracting States result or will result for him in taxation not in accordance with the provisions of this Convention, he may, irrespective of the remedies provided by the domestic law of those States, and the time limits prescribed in such laws for presenting claims for refund, present his case to the competent authority of either Contracting State.

2. The competent authority shall endeavor, if the objection appears to it to be justified and if it is not itself able to arrive at a satisfactory solution, to resolve the case by mutual agreement with the competent authority of the other Contracting State, with a view to the avoidance of taxation which is not in accordance with the Convention. Any agreement reached shall be implemented notwithstanding any time limits or other procedural limitations in the domestic law of the Contracting States. Assessment and collection procedures shall be suspended during the pendency of any mutual agreement proceeding.

3. The competent authorities of the Contracting States shall endeavor to resolve by mutual agreement any difficulties or doubts arising as to the interpretation or application of the Convention. In particular the competent authorities of the Contracting States may agree:

a) to the same attribution of income, deductions, credits, or allowances of an enterprise of a Contracting State to its permanent establishment situated in the other Contracting State;

b) to the same allocation of income, deductions, credits, or allowances between persons;

c) to the same characterization of particular items of income, including the same characterization of income that is assimilated to income from shares by the taxation law of one of the Contracting States and that is treated as a different class of income in the other State;

d) to the same characterization of persons;

e) to the same application of source rules with respect to particular items of income;

f) to a common meaning of a term;

g) to advance pricing arrangements; and

h) to the application of the provisions of domestic law regarding penalties, fines, and interest in a manner consistent with the purposes of the Convention.

They may also consult together for the elimination of double taxation in cases not provided for in the Convention.

4. The competent authorities also may agree to increases in any specific dollar amounts referred to in the Convention to reflect economic or monetary developments.

5. The competent authorities of the Contracting States may communicate with each other directly for the purpose of reaching an agreement in the sense of the preceding paragraphs.

1996 U.S. Model
Income Tax Convention

Article 26

EXCHANGE OF INFORMATION AND ADMINISTRATIVE ASSISTANCE

1. The competent authorities of the Contracting States shall exchange such information as is relevant for carrying out the provisions of this Convention or of the domestic laws of the Contracting States concerning taxes covered by the Convention insofar as the taxation thereunder is not contrary to the Convention, including information relating to the assessment or collection of, the enforcement or prosecution in respect of, or the determination of appeals in relation to, the taxes covered by the Convention. The exchange of information is not restricted by Article 1 (General Scope). Any information received by a Contracting State shall be treated as secret in the same manner as information obtained under the domestic laws of that State and shall be disclosed only to persons or authorities (including courts and administrative bodies) involved in the assessment, collection, or administration of, the enforcement or prosecution in respect of, or the determination of appeals in relation to, the taxes covered by the Convention or the oversight of the above. Such persons or authorities shall use the information only for such purposes. They may disclose the information in public court proceedings or in judicial decisions.

2. In no case shall the provisions of paragraph 1 be construed so as to impose on a Contracting State the obligation:

    a) to carry out administrative measures at variance with the laws and administrative practice of that or of the other Contracting State;

    b) to supply information that is not obtainable under the laws or in the normal course of the administration of that or of the other Contracting State;

    c) to supply information that would disclose any trade, business, industrial, commercial, or professional secret or trade process, or information the disclosure of which would be contrary to public policy (ordre public).

3. Notwithstanding paragraph 2, the competent authority of the requested State shall have the authority to obtain and provide information held by financial institutions, nominees or persons acting in an agency or fiduciary capacity, or respecting interests in a person, including bearer shares, regardless of any

1996 U.S. Model
Income Tax Convention

laws or practices of the requested State that might otherwise preclude the obtaining of such information. If information is requested by a Contracting State in accordance with this Article, the other Contracting State shall obtain that information in the same manner and to the same extent as if the tax of the first-mentioned State were the tax of that other State and were being imposed by that other State, notwithstanding that the other State may not, at that time, need such information for purposes of its own tax. If specifically requested by the competent authority of a Contracting State, the competent authority of the other Contracting State shall provide information under this Article in the form of depositions of witnesses and authenticated copies of unedited original documents (including books, papers, statements, records, accounts, and writings), to the same extent such depositions and documents can be obtained under the laws and administrative practices of that other State with respect to its own taxes.

4. Each of the Contracting States shall endeavor to collect on behalf of the other Contracting State such amounts as may be necessary to ensure that relief granted by the Convention from taxation imposed by that other State does not inure to the benefit of persons not entitled thereto. This paragraph shall not impose upon either of the Contracting States the obligation to carry out administrative measures that would be contrary to its sovereignty, security, or public policy.

5. For the purposes of this Article, the Convention shall apply, notwithstanding the provisions of Article 2 (Taxes Covered), to taxes of every kind imposed by a Contracting State.

6. The competent authority of the requested State shall allow representatives of the applicant State to enter the requested State to interview individuals and examine books and records with the consent of the persons subject to examination.

Article 27

DIPLOMATIC AGENTS AND CONSULAR OFFICERS

Nothing in this Convention shall affect the fiscal privileges of diplomatic agents or consular officers under the general rules of international law or under the provisions of special agreements.

1996 U.S. Model
Income Tax Convention

Article 28

ENTRY INTO FORCE

1. This Convention shall be subject to ratification in accordance with the applicable procedures of each Contracting State. Each Contracting State shall notify the other as soon as its procedures have been complied with.

2. The Convention shall enter into force on the date of the receipt of the later of such notifications, and its provisions shall have effect:

    a) in respect of taxes withheld at source, for amounts paid or credited on or after the first day of the second month next following the date on which the Convention enters into force;

    b) in respect of other taxes, for taxable periods beginning on or after the first day of January next following the date on which the Convention enters into force.

1996 U.S. Model
Income Tax Convention

Article 29

TERMINATION

1. This Convention shall remain in force until terminated by a Contracting State. Either Contracting State may terminate the Convention by giving notice of termination to the other Contracting State through diplomatic channels. In such event, the Convention shall cease to have effect:

    a) in respect of taxes withheld at source, for amounts paid or credited after the expiration of the 6 month period beginning on the date on which notice of termination was given; and

    b) in respect of other taxes, for taxable periods beginning on or after the expiration of the 6 month period beginning on the date on which notice of termination was given.

IN WITNESS WHEREOF, the undersigned, being duly authorized thereto by their respective Governments, have signed this Convention.

DONE at _____ in duplicate, in the English and _____ languages, both texts being equally authentic, this ____ day of (month) , 19__.

FOR THE UNITED STATES   FOR: _____
OF AMERICA:

www.ingramcontent.com/pod-product-compliance
Lightning Source LLC
Chambersburg PA
CBHW081801170526
45167CB00008B/3274